EMMANUEL JOSEPH

The Robotic Gourmet, How Technology and Sociology Are Redefining the Culinary World

Copyright © 2025 by Emmanuel Joseph

All rights reserved. No part of this publication may be reproduced, stored or transmitted in any form or by any means, electronic, mechanical, photocopying, recording, scanning, or otherwise without written permission from the publisher. It is illegal to copy this book, post it to a website, or distribute it by any other means without permission.

First edition

This book was professionally typeset on Reedsy. Find out more at reedsy.com

Contents

1. Chapter 1: The Dawn of Technological Culinary Innovation — 1
2. Chapter 2: The Social Dynamics of Dining in the Digital Age — 3
3. Chapter 3: Culinary Education in the Era of Technology — 5
4. Chapter 4: The Intersection of Tradition and Innovation — 7
5. Chapter 5: The Rise of Plant-Based and Alternative Proteins — 9
6. Chapter 6: The Future of Food Sustainability — 11
7. Chapter 7: The Impact of Food Delivery and Automation — 13
8. Chapter 8: The Role of AI in Culinary Creativity — 15
9. Chapter 9: The Evolution of Food Culture in a Globalized... — 17
10. Chapter 10: The Influence of Technology on Food Safety and... — 19
11. Chapter 11: The Ethical Considerations of Technological... — 21
12. Chapter 12: The Future of Culinary Innovation — 23
13. Chapter 13: The Role of Robotics in Culinary Arts — 25
14. Chapter 14: The Influence of Technology on Global Food... — 27
15. Chapter 15: The Role of Technology in Culinary Education and... — 29
16. Chapter 16: The Impact of Social Media on Culinary Trends — 31
17. Chapter 17: The Role of Technology in Sustainable Food... — 33

1

Chapter 1: The Dawn of Technological Culinary Innovation

In recent years, technology has infiltrated every facet of our lives, including the culinary world. The advent of smart kitchen appliances has revolutionized how we cook and interact with food. Devices such as smart ovens, thermomixers, and Wi-Fi-enabled refrigerators have transformed the home kitchen into an interconnected ecosystem, where precision cooking and convenience reign supreme. These technological advancements not only streamline the cooking process but also democratize gourmet cooking, making it accessible to everyday home cooks who may not have formal culinary training.

At the heart of this revolution is the concept of the "Internet of Things" (IoT), which enables kitchen devices to communicate with each other and with us. Imagine a refrigerator that can track the freshness of your ingredients and suggest recipes based on what you have on hand. Or an oven that can be preheated remotely through a smartphone app, ensuring that dinner is ready the moment you walk through the door. These innovations are not just about convenience; they also promote sustainability by reducing food waste and optimizing energy use.

Robots have also made their way into professional kitchens, taking on repetitive and labor-intensive tasks. From robotic arms that can flawlessly chop vegetables to machines that can prepare complex dishes with precision, these advancements are reshaping the role of chefs. While some fear that robots may replace human chefs, others argue that they will instead augment their capabilities, allowing them to focus on creativity and innovation.

Moreover, artificial intelligence (AI) is playing a significant role in personalized nutrition and dietary planning. AI-powered apps can analyze an individual's dietary preferences, health goals, and even genetic information to create tailored meal plans. This level of customization ensures that individuals receive the nutrients they need while enjoying meals that cater to their tastes and lifestyle. As we move forward, the integration of technology in the culinary world promises to bring even more exciting developments.

2

Chapter 2: The Social Dynamics of Dining in the Digital Age

The way we dine and socialize around food has undergone a significant transformation in the digital age. Social media platforms have become virtual dining rooms, where people share their culinary experiences, discover new recipes, and connect with food enthusiasts from around the world. The rise of food bloggers, influencers, and YouTube chefs has democratized the dissemination of culinary knowledge, allowing anyone with an internet connection to learn new cooking techniques and explore global cuisines.

Food photography has become an art form in its own right, with Instagram-worthy dishes driving culinary trends and restaurant choices. Restaurants and chefs are acutely aware of the power of social media and often design their menus and plating styles with visual appeal in mind. This phenomenon has given rise to the term "foodstagramming," where diners photograph their meals and share them online before taking a single bite. While some critics argue that this trend detracts from the traditional dining experience, others see it as a way to celebrate and share the beauty of food.

Virtual and augmented reality technologies are also changing the way we experience food. Virtual reality (VR) dining experiences allow individuals to "travel" to different parts of the world and enjoy meals in immersive environments. Imagine dining on a beach in Bali or in a quaint Parisian café, all from the comfort of your home. Augmented reality (AR) menus, on the other hand, provide interactive and dynamic information about dishes, including ingredient sourcing, nutritional content, and preparation methods. These technologies not only enhance the dining experience but also educate consumers about the food they are eating.

The digital age has also given rise to new dining concepts, such as ghost kitchens and food delivery apps. Ghost kitchens are commercial cooking spaces that cater exclusively to online orders, eliminating the need for a physical dining space. This model allows for greater flexibility and efficiency in food production and delivery. Food delivery apps, powered by algorithms and AI, provide personalized recommendations and seamless ordering experiences. These innovations have not only changed the way we dine but also challenged traditional restaurant models.

3

Chapter 3: Culinary Education in the Era of Technology

The landscape of culinary education has evolved dramatically with the integration of technology. Traditional culinary schools and apprenticeships are no longer the sole pathways to becoming a skilled chef. Online platforms and virtual cooking classes have made culinary education more accessible and flexible, catering to diverse learning styles and schedules. Aspiring chefs can now learn from renowned instructors, access a wealth of resources, and practice their skills from the comfort of their own kitchens.

Interactive cooking tutorials and video demonstrations have become valuable tools for learning. Platforms like YouTube, MasterClass, and Skillshare offer a wide range of cooking classes, from basic techniques to advanced culinary artistry. These platforms allow learners to pause, rewind, and practice at their own pace, fostering a deeper understanding of the material. Additionally, virtual cooking competitions and challenges provide opportunities for aspiring chefs to showcase their skills and receive feedback from industry professionals.

Artificial intelligence is also making its mark on culinary education. AI-powered recipe generators and virtual sous-chefs can assist learners in experimenting with new ingredients and techniques. These tools provide real-time guidance and suggestions, helping individuals build confidence and creativity in the kitchen. Furthermore, AI can analyze learners' progress and tailor recommendations to their skill level and interests, creating a personalized learning experience.

Beyond technical skills, technology is also enhancing the understanding of food science and nutrition. Online courses and apps offer in-depth knowledge of the chemical and biological processes behind cooking, as well as the impact of different ingredients on health. This holistic approach to culinary education equips future chefs with the knowledge to create not only delicious but also nutritious and sustainable meals. As technology continues to advance, the possibilities for culinary education are boundless.

4

Chapter 4: The Intersection of Tradition and Innovation

While technology is reshaping the culinary world, it is important to recognize the enduring value of tradition. Many chefs and culinary enthusiasts strive to balance innovation with the preservation of cultural heritage and time-honored techniques. This intersection of tradition and technology creates a dynamic and evolving culinary landscape that celebrates both the past and the future.

Traditional cooking methods and recipes are being documented and preserved through digital platforms. Websites, blogs, and social media channels dedicated to culinary heritage allow individuals to share their family recipes and cultural practices with a global audience. This digital archive ensures that traditional knowledge is passed down to future generations, even as new technologies emerge.

Innovative chefs are also finding ways to incorporate traditional ingredients and techniques into modern cuisine. Molecular gastronomy, for example, combines the principles of food science with traditional culinary practices to create unique and unexpected dishes. Techniques such as sous-vide cooking, which involves vacuum-sealing food and cooking it at precise temperatures, draw inspiration from traditional preservation methods while utilizing modern technology.

Moreover, technology is enhancing the preservation and sustainability of traditional ingredients. Genetic mapping and seed banks are being used to protect heirloom varieties of fruits, vegetables, and grains. Vertical farming and hydroponics allow for the cultivation of crops in urban environments, ensuring a steady supply of fresh ingredients while reducing the environmental impact. These innovations not only support traditional agricultural practices but also promote food security and sustainability.

In conclusion, the culinary world is at a fascinating crossroads where tradition and innovation coexist and enrich each other. As technology continues to advance, it is essential to honor the cultural and historical significance of food while embracing the opportunities for creativity and progress. This delicate balance ensures that the culinary world remains vibrant, diverse, and ever-evolving.

5

Chapter 5: The Rise of Plant-Based and Alternative Proteins

The global demand for sustainable and ethical food choices has led to the rise of plant-based and alternative proteins. Technology and sociology play crucial roles in this culinary revolution, as consumers become more conscious of the environmental and health impacts of their food choices. Plant-based diets are no longer limited to a niche market; they have entered the mainstream, driven by advancements in food science and a growing awareness of sustainability.

The development of plant-based meat alternatives, such as those offered by companies like Beyond Meat and Impossible Foods, has revolutionized the way we perceive and consume protein. These products are designed to mimic the taste, texture, and appearance of traditional meat, providing a familiar experience for consumers while reducing the environmental footprint. The use of innovative ingredients, such as pea protein, soy, and heme, has enabled the creation of plant-based products that are both nutritious and satisfying.

In addition to plant-based meats, alternative proteins from sources such as algae, insects, and lab-grown meat are gaining traction. Algae, for example, is a highly sustainable protein source that can be cultivated in various environments and has minimal environmental impact. Insects, which are already consumed in many cultures around the world, are being promoted as a sustainable and nutrient-dense protein option. Lab-grown meat, also known as cultured meat, is produced by culturing animal cells in a controlled environment, offering the potential to produce meat without the need for traditional animal farming.

Sociologically, the shift towards plant-based and alternative proteins reflects changing attitudes towards food and sustainability. Consumers are increasingly seeking out ethical and environmentally friendly food choices, driven by a desire to reduce their carbon footprint and support animal welfare. This trend is also influenced by the rise of social media and the availability of information, which has made consumers more aware of the impact of their food choices.

As technology continues to advance, the potential for innovation in plant-based and alternative proteins is limitless. Scientists and food technologists are exploring new ways to enhance the taste, texture, and nutritional profile of these products, making them even more appealing to a wider audience. The rise of plant-based and alternative proteins is not just a trend; it is a fundamental shift in the way we think about and consume food.

6

Chapter 6: The Future of Food Sustainability

The quest for sustainable food systems is one of the most pressing challenges of our time. Technology and sociology are at the forefront of this endeavor, driving innovations that aim to reduce the environmental impact of food production and consumption. From farm to table, every stage of the food supply chain is being reimagined to promote sustainability and resilience.

Precision agriculture is one such innovation. By utilizing GPS, IoT sensors, and data analytics, farmers can monitor and manage their crops with unprecedented accuracy. These technologies allow for the efficient use of resources, such as water and fertilizers, reducing waste and environmental impact. Drones and autonomous tractors are also being used to perform tasks such as planting, spraying, and harvesting, further optimizing the agricultural process. These advancements not only increase productivity but also promote sustainable farming practices.

In urban areas, vertical farming and hydroponics are gaining popularity as solutions to the challenges of traditional agriculture. Vertical farms use stacked layers to grow crops in a controlled environment, allowing for year-round production and reducing the need for pesticides and herbicides. Hydroponics, which involves growing plants in nutrient-rich water rather than soil, also offers a sustainable alternative. These methods require less land and water, making them ideal for urban environments where space is limited.

Food waste is another critical issue that technology is addressing. AI-powered apps and platforms are being developed to help consumers and businesses reduce food waste. These tools can track expiration dates, suggest recipes based on leftover ingredients, and connect surplus food with those in need. Additionally, advancements in packaging technology, such as biodegradable and edible packaging, are reducing the environmental impact of food packaging waste.

On the sociological front, there is a growing movement towards mindful and conscious consumption. Consumers are increasingly aware of the environmental and ethical implications of their food choices and are seeking out sustainable and ethical options. This shift in consumer behavior is driving demand for sustainably produced and sourced foods, encouraging businesses to adopt more sustainable practices. Educational campaigns and initiatives are also raising awareness about the importance of food sustainability, empowering individuals to make informed choices.

In conclusion, the future of food sustainability lies at the intersection of technology and sociology. By leveraging technological innovations and fostering a culture of mindful consumption, we can create a more sustainable and resilient food system. As we continue to face global challenges such as climate change and population growth, these efforts are essential to ensuring food security and the well-being of future generations.

7

Chapter 7: The Impact of Food Delivery and Automation

The rise of food delivery services and automation has fundamentally changed the way we access and consume food. The convenience of ordering meals with just a few taps on a smartphone has become an integral part of modern life. Companies like Uber Eats, DoorDash, and Grubhub have revolutionized the food delivery industry, offering a vast array of culinary options at our fingertips. This shift towards on-demand food delivery is reshaping the culinary landscape, impacting restaurants, consumers, and the workforce.

Automation is playing a significant role in the food delivery process, from order placement to food preparation and delivery. AI-powered algorithms optimize delivery routes, ensuring that food arrives quickly and efficiently. Autonomous delivery vehicles, such as drones and robots, are being tested and implemented in various cities, reducing the need for human delivery drivers and minimizing the environmental impact of food transportation. These technologies are not only enhancing the speed and efficiency of food delivery but also reducing costs for businesses and consumers.

In the realm of food preparation, automation is making its mark with the advent of robotic kitchens and automated cooking devices. Robotic chefs, such as Flippy the burger-flipping robot and Sally the salad-making robot, are capable of preparing dishes with precision and consistency. These machines can work tirelessly, reducing labor costs and increasing productivity in commercial kitchens. While some fear that automation may lead to job displacement, others argue that it can alleviate labor shortages and allow human workers to focus on more creative and complex tasks.

The convenience of food delivery and automation has also led to changes in consumer behavior. Busy lifestyles and the desire for convenience have increased the demand for ready-to-eat meals and takeout options. This shift has prompted restaurants to adapt their menus and operations to cater to delivery and takeout customers. Many establishments are now offering delivery-exclusive menus, meal kits, and virtual dining experiences to meet the evolving needs of their clientele.

Moreover, the rise of food delivery and automation has sparked discussions about the future of dining and the role of technology in our daily lives. As these trends continue to evolve, it is essential to consider their social and economic implications and to ensure that they contribute to a more equitable and sustainable food system.

8

Chapter 8: The Role of AI in Culinary Creativity

Artificial intelligence (AI) is not only revolutionizing the technical aspects of cooking but also inspiring new levels of culinary creativity. AI-powered tools and platforms are assisting chefs and home cooks in experimenting with ingredients, flavors, and techniques, pushing the boundaries of what is possible in the kitchen.

One of the most notable examples of AI in culinary creativity is IBM's Chef Watson, an AI system designed to generate unique and innovative recipes. Chef Watson analyzes vast amounts of data, including ingredient combinations, flavor profiles, and cultural preferences, to create novel dishes that might not have been conceived by human chefs. This technology allows chefs to explore new culinary territories and discover unexpected flavor pairings that can delight and surprise diners.

AI is also being used to analyze and predict food trends. By processing data from social media, restaurant reviews, and consumer behavior, AI can identify emerging trends and preferences, helping chefs and food businesses stay ahead of the curve. This insight enables culinary professionals to innovate and adapt their offerings to meet the ever-changing demands of the market.

In addition to generating recipes and predicting trends, AI is enhancing the dining experience through personalized recommendations and interactive menus. AI-powered apps and platforms can analyze an individual's taste preferences, dietary restrictions, and eating habits to provide tailored meal suggestions. Interactive menus, equipped with AI, can offer dynamic information about dishes, including ingredient sourcing, nutritional content, and preparation methods. These personalized experiences not only enhance customer satisfaction but also promote informed and mindful eating.

Furthermore, AI is being used to create immersive and multisensory dining experiences. Virtual and augmented reality technologies, powered by AI, allow diners to embark on culinary journeys that engage all their senses. From virtual cooking classes to immersive dining experiences that transport diners to different parts of the world, AI is opening up new possibilities for culinary exploration and enjoyment.

In conclusion, AI is playing a pivotal role in shaping the future of culinary creativity. By providing chefs and home cooks with innovative tools and insights, AI is fostering a new era of experimentation and discovery in the kitchen. As technology continues to advance, the potential for AI-driven culinary innovation is boundless, promising exciting developments for food lovers everywhere.

9

Chapter 9: The Evolution of Food Culture in a Globalized World

Globalization has brought about profound changes in food culture, as culinary traditions and practices from around the world intersect and influence one another. Technology and sociology are key drivers of this cultural exchange, enabling people to discover, share, and experience global cuisines like never before.

The proliferation of international food media, including television shows, cookbooks, and online platforms, has introduced diverse culinary traditions to a global audience. Chefs and food enthusiasts are increasingly drawing inspiration from different cultures, incorporating elements from various cuisines into their own creations. This fusion of flavors and techniques has given rise to innovative dishes that celebrate the richness of global culinary heritage.

Social media has played a significant role in the globalization of food culture. Platforms like Instagram, YouTube, and TikTok allow individuals to share their culinary experiences and discoveries with a global audience. Food bloggers, influencers, and content creators showcase dishes from around the world, inspiring others to try new recipes and explore different cuisines. This digital exchange of culinary knowledge has created a sense of interconnectedness and appreciation for the diversity of food.

The rise of global food trends is another manifestation of the impact of globalization on food culture. Trends such as sushi burritos, Korean barbecue, and bubble tea have gained popularity beyond their countries of origin, becoming global phenomena. These trends reflect the dynamic nature of food culture, as people adopt and adapt culinary practices to suit their tastes and preferences. The globalization of food has also led to the creation of new culinary traditions that blend elements from multiple cultures.

However, the globalization of food culture also raises important questions about cultural appropriation and authenticity. As culinary practices are adopted and adapted across borders, it is essential to acknowledge and respect the cultural significance of these traditions. Culinary professionals and enthusiasts must strive to honor the origins and heritage of the dishes they create and enjoy, promoting a deeper understanding and appreciation of global food culture.

In conclusion, the globalization of food culture is a testament to the power of technology and sociology in fostering cultural exchange and innovation. As we continue to explore and celebrate the diversity of food, it is important to approach this cultural exchange with respect and mindfulness, ensuring that the rich tapestry of global culinary traditions is preserved and honored.

10

Chapter 10: The Influence of Technology on Food Safety and Quality

Ensuring food safety and quality is a critical aspect of the culinary world, and technology is playing an increasingly important role in this endeavor. From farm to fork, technological advancements are enhancing the ability to monitor, trace, and control the safety and quality of food products, protecting consumers and promoting public health.

One of the key innovations in food safety is blockchain technology. Blockchain provides a secure and transparent way to track the journey of food products through the supply chain. By recording every transaction and movement of a product, blockchain ensures the traceability and authenticity of food items, reducing the risk of fraud and contamination. Consumers can access detailed information about the origin and handling of their food, fostering trust and confidence in the products they purchase.

Sensor technology is also making a significant impact on food safety. IoT sensors are being used to monitor temperature, humidity, and other environmental conditions during the storage and transportation of food. These sensors provide real-time data, Sensor technology is also making a significant impact on food safety. IoT sensors are being used to monitor temperature, humidity, and other environmental conditions during the storage and transportation of food. These sensors provide real-time data, allowing for the immediate identification and resolution of potential issues. For example, if a shipment of perishable goods exceeds the optimal temperature range, alerts can be sent to the relevant parties to take corrective action. This proactive approach helps prevent spoilage and ensures that food products reach consumers in optimal condition.

Another technological advancement in food safety is the use of DNA testing to verify the authenticity and safety of food products. DNA-based methods can identify the species of animals and plants used in food products, detect contaminants, and verify labeling claims. This level of precision enhances the ability to identify and address food fraud and adulteration, protecting consumers from potentially harmful products.

Food quality is also being improved through the use of technology. Advanced imaging and spectroscopy techniques are being employed to assess the quality of food products, such as determining the ripeness of fruits, the freshness of seafood, and the presence of foreign substances. These non-invasive methods provide accurate and reliable assessments, reducing the reliance on manual inspection and subjective judgment.

Furthermore, technology is enhancing the ability to trace and recall food products in the event of a safety issue. Traceability systems, powered by blockchain and other technologies, provide a clear and detailed record of the journey of food products through the supply chain. This transparency allows for the quick identification and removal of contaminated or unsafe products, minimizing the risk to consumers and maintaining public trust in the food system.

In conclusion, technology is playing a vital role in ensuring the safety and quality of food products. By leveraging advancements in blockchain, IoT sensors, DNA testing, and traceability systems, the culinary world can provide consumers with safe, high-quality, and trustworthy food. As these technologies continue to evolve, they will further enhance our ability to protect public health and maintain the integrity of the food supply.

11

Chapter 11: The Ethical Considerations of Technological Advancements in Food

As technology continues to shape the culinary world, it is essential to consider the ethical implications of these advancements. From the impact on employment to issues of accessibility and equity, the integration of technology in food production and consumption raises important questions that must be addressed.

One of the primary ethical concerns is the potential displacement of workers due to automation. While technological advancements can increase efficiency and productivity, they may also lead to job loss in certain sectors. For example, the use of robotic chefs and automated food delivery systems could reduce the need for human labor in commercial kitchens and delivery services. It is crucial to consider how these changes will impact workers and to explore ways to support them in transitioning to new roles or industries.

Another ethical consideration is the accessibility of technology-driven culinary innovations. While advancements such as smart kitchen appliances and personalized nutrition apps offer numerous benefits, they may not be accessible to everyone. The cost of these technologies and the digital divide can create disparities in who can take advantage of these innovations. Ensuring that technological advancements are inclusive and accessible to all is essential for promoting equity in the culinary world.

The environmental impact of technological advancements is also an important ethical consideration. While many innovations aim to promote sustainability, it is essential to evaluate their overall environmental footprint. For example, the production and disposal of electronic devices can contribute to e-waste and resource depletion. Balancing the benefits of technology with its environmental impact requires thoughtful consideration and the development of sustainable practices.

Furthermore, the ethical treatment of animals in food production is a significant concern. While lab-grown meat and plant-based alternatives offer ethical and sustainable options, traditional animal farming practices often raise questions about animal welfare. The adoption of technologies that prioritize humane and sustainable practices is crucial for addressing these ethical issues.

In conclusion, the ethical considerations of technological advancements in food are complex and multifaceted. As the culinary world continues to evolve, it is essential to address these concerns and strive for solutions that promote fairness, inclusivity, and sustainability. By doing so, we can ensure that the benefits of technology are shared equitably and responsibly.

12

Chapter 12: The Future of Culinary Innovation

The future of culinary innovation is poised to be even more dynamic and exciting, with technology and sociology continuing to drive transformative changes. As we look ahead, several emerging trends and developments promise to reshape the culinary landscape in unprecedented ways.

One of the most promising areas of innovation is the use of artificial intelligence and machine learning to create hyper-personalized dining experiences. AI-powered algorithms can analyze a vast array of data, including individual preferences, dietary restrictions, and even genetic information, to craft tailored meal plans and recipes. This level of personalization ensures that individuals receive not only delicious but also nutritionally optimized meals that cater to their unique needs and tastes.

The integration of biotechnology and food science is also set to revolutionize the culinary world. Advances in genetic engineering and fermentation technology are enabling the development of novel food products with enhanced nutritional profiles and environmental benefits. For example, bioengineered crops with increased resistance to pests and diseases can reduce the need for chemical pesticides, while fermentation-derived ingredients can offer sustainable alternatives to traditional animal-based products.

The rise of immersive dining experiences is another exciting trend. Virtual and augmented reality technologies are enabling diners to embark on multisensory culinary journeys that engage all their senses. From interactive cooking classes to virtual dining environments that transport diners to different parts of the world, these experiences offer new and imaginative ways to enjoy food.

Sociologically, the future of culinary innovation will continue to be shaped by changing consumer preferences and cultural dynamics. The growing emphasis on sustainability, health, and ethical considerations will drive demand for food products and practices that align with these values. Additionally, the increasing interconnectedness of the global food community will foster the exchange of culinary knowledge and traditions, leading to the creation of new and exciting culinary fusions.

In conclusion, the future of culinary innovation is bright and full of possibilities. By harnessing the power of technology and embracing the dynamic nature of food culture, we can look forward to a culinary landscape that is more diverse, sustainable, and enjoyable than ever before. As we navigate this exciting journey, it is essential to remain mindful of the ethical and environmental implications of our choices and to strive for a future that celebrates the richness and beauty of food in all its forms.

13

Chapter 13: The Role of Robotics in Culinary Arts

Robotics is revolutionizing the culinary arts in ways that were once thought to be science fiction. Robotic arms, automated cooking stations, and intelligent kitchen assistants are becoming increasingly common in both professional and home kitchens. These advanced machines are capable of performing complex tasks with precision and consistency, taking on roles that were traditionally reserved for human chefs.

In professional kitchens, robots are being used to streamline operations and enhance efficiency. Robotic arms can handle tasks such as chopping, stirring, and plating, ensuring that each dish is prepared to perfection. These machines can work tirelessly, reducing the physical strain on human workers and allowing chefs to focus on creative and managerial aspects of their craft. Additionally, robots can operate in environments that are hazardous or uncomfortable for humans, such as extreme temperatures or confined spaces.

Home kitchens are also benefiting from robotic innovations. Smart appliances equipped with robotic technology can assist home cooks in various ways, from preparing ingredients to cooking entire meals. For example, robotic sous-chefs can follow recipes step-by-step, ensuring that dishes are cooked to exact specifications. This level of automation not only makes cooking more accessible but also allows home cooks to experiment with complex techniques and recipes that they might not have attempted otherwise.

The integration of robotics in the culinary arts raises questions about the future of the profession. While some fear that robots may replace human chefs, others see them as valuable tools that can enhance human creativity and innovation. By taking on repetitive and labor-intensive tasks, robots can free up chefs to focus on experimentation and artistic expression. This collaborative approach between humans and robots has the potential to push the boundaries of culinary arts to new heights.

14

Chapter 14: The Influence of Technology on Global Food Security

Ensuring global food security is one of the most critical challenges facing humanity, and technology is playing a crucial role in addressing this issue. From improving agricultural productivity to enhancing food distribution and storage, technological advancements are helping to ensure that people around the world have access to safe, nutritious, and affordable food.

One of the key innovations in this area is precision agriculture. By leveraging GPS, IoT sensors, and data analytics, farmers can optimize their use of resources such as water, fertilizers, and pesticides. This not only increases crop yields but also reduces environmental impact and ensures that food is produced more sustainably. Drones and autonomous farming equipment are also being used to monitor crop health, detect pests, and apply treatments with pinpoint accuracy, further enhancing agricultural efficiency.

Another important development is the use of biotechnology to create resilient and high-yielding crops. Genetic engineering and CRISPR technology are enabling scientists to develop crops that are resistant to diseases, pests, and environmental stresses such as drought and salinity. These innovations have the potential to significantly increase food production in regions that are vulnerable to climate change and other challenges.

Food storage and distribution are also being transformed by technology. Smart storage solutions equipped with sensors and data analytics can monitor and maintain optimal conditions for food preservation, reducing spoilage and waste. Blockchain technology is being used to create transparent and secure supply chains, ensuring that food products are traceable from farm to fork. This not only enhances food safety but also helps to prevent fraud and ensure that consumers receive authentic and high-quality products.

In conclusion, technology is playing a vital role in enhancing global food security. By improving agricultural productivity, enhancing food storage and distribution, and developing resilient crops, technological advancements are helping to ensure that people around the world have access to safe and nutritious food. As we continue to face global challenges such as climate change and population growth, these innovations are essential for building a sustainable and resilient food system.

15

Chapter 15: The Role of Technology in Culinary Education and Training

The landscape of culinary education and training has undergone a significant transformation with the integration of technology. Traditional culinary schools and apprenticeships are being complemented by online platforms, virtual classes, and interactive learning tools, making culinary education more accessible and flexible than ever before.

One of the key advancements in this area is the availability of online cooking classes and tutorials. Platforms such as YouTube, MasterClass, and Skillshare offer a wide range of cooking lessons, from basic techniques to advanced culinary artistry. These platforms provide learners with the flexibility to learn at their own pace and practice their skills from the comfort of their own kitchens. Interactive video demonstrations and step-by-step tutorials make it easier for aspiring chefs to understand and master various cooking techniques.

Virtual reality (VR) and augmented reality (AR) technologies are also making their way into culinary education. VR cooking classes offer immersive learning experiences, allowing students to virtually step into a professional kitchen and learn from renowned chefs. AR applications can provide real-time guidance and feedback as students practice their cooking skills, overlaying instructions and tips onto the physical environment. These technologies enhance the learning experience by providing hands-on practice and immediate feedback.

Artificial intelligence (AI) is another powerful tool in culinary education. AI-powered recipe generators and virtual sous-chefs can assist learners in experimenting with new ingredients and techniques. These tools provide real-time guidance and suggestions, helping individuals build confidence and creativity in the kitchen. Additionally, AI can analyze learners' progress and tailor recommendations to their skill level and interests, creating a personalized learning experience.

In conclusion, technology is revolutionizing culinary education and training. By making learning more accessible, interactive, and personalized, technological advancements are equipping aspiring chefs with the skills and knowledge they need to succeed in the culinary world. As technology continues to evolve, the possibilities for culinary education are boundless, promising exciting developments for future generations of chefs.

16

Chapter 16: The Impact of Social Media on Culinary Trends

Social media has had a profound impact on culinary trends, shaping the way we discover, share, and experience food. Platforms such as Instagram, YouTube, and TikTok have become virtual dining rooms, where food enthusiasts from around the world connect and share their culinary creations. The influence of social media on the culinary world is undeniable, driving trends and shaping consumer behavior in unprecedented ways.

One of the most significant effects of social media is the rise of food influencers and bloggers. These individuals have amassed large followings by sharing their culinary adventures, recipes, and reviews. Their influence extends beyond social media, as their recommendations and endorsements can drive traffic to restaurants, boost sales of food products, and even inspire new culinary trends. Food influencers have democratized the dissemination of culinary knowledge, allowing anyone with an internet connection to learn new cooking techniques and explore global cuisines.

Food photography has also become an art form in its own right, with Instagram-worthy dishes driving culinary trends and restaurant choices. Restaurants and chefs are acutely aware of the power of social media and often design their menus and plating styles with visual appeal in mind. This phenomenon has given rise to the term "foodstagramming," where diners photograph their meals and share them online before taking a single bite. While some critics argue that this trend detracts from the traditional dining experience, others see it as a way to celebrate and share the beauty of food.

Social media has also facilitated the rapid spread of food trends and innovations. Viral food challenges, unique recipes, and creative food combinations can gain widespread attention and influence culinary practices worldwide. Trends such as avocado toast, rainbow-colored foods, and Dalgona coffee have captured the collective imagination of social media users, driving demand and inspiring new culinary creations. The speed at which these trends emerge and evolve is a testament to the power of social media in shaping the culinary landscape.

In conclusion, social media has had a transformative impact on culinary trends. By providing a platform for food enthusiasts to connect, share, and inspire, social media has democratized culinary knowledge and driven innovation in the culinary world. As social media continues to evolve, its influence on the way we experience and enjoy food is likely to grow, shaping the future of culinary trends in exciting and unpredictable ways.

17

Chapter 17: The Role of Technology in Sustainable Food Practices

Sustainability is a growing concern in the culinary world, and technology is playing a crucial role in promoting sustainable food practices. From reducing food waste to optimizing resource use, technological advancements are helping to create a more sustainable and environmentally friendly food system.

One of the key areas where technology is making a significant impact is in the reduction of food waste. AI-powered apps and platforms are being developed to help consumers and businesses track and manage food inventory, reducing the amount of food that goes to waste. These tools can suggest recipes based on leftover ingredients, monitor expiration dates, and connect surplus food with those in need. By leveraging data and analytics, technology is helping to minimize food waste and promote more efficient use of resources.

Sustainable farming practices are also being enhanced by technology. Precision agriculture, which involves the use of IoT sensors, GPS, and data analytics, allows farmers to monitor and manage their crops with greater accuracy. This technology enables the efficient use of water, fertilizers, and pesticides, reducing the environmental impact of farming. Additionally, vertical farming and hydroponics offer sustainable alternatives to traditional agriculture, allowing for the cultivation of crops in urban environments with minimal resource use.

In the realm of food production, technology is enabling the development of sustainable and ethical alternatives to traditional animal-based products. Plant-based meats and dairy alternatives are becoming increasingly popular, driven by advancements in food science and technology. These products offer a more sustainable and humane option for consumers who want to reduce their environmental footprint. Lab-grown meat, also known as cultured meat, is another promising innovation that has the potential to revolutionize the way we produce and consume protein.

Packaging technology is also playing a role in promoting sustainability. Biodegradable and edible packaging solutions are being developed to reduce the environmental impact of food packaging waste. Innovations such as plant-based plastics, compostable materials, and edible coatings offer sustainable alternatives to traditional packaging, minimizing the environmental footprint of food products.

The Robotic Gourmet: How Technology and Sociology Are Redefining the Culinary World

In an era where technology touches every aspect of our lives, "The Robotic Gourmet" delves into the fascinating intersection of technology, sociology, and culinary arts. This book explores how innovations such as artificial intelligence, robotics, and social media are reshaping the way we cook, dine, and think about food. It looks at the impact of smart kitchen appliances, the role of AI in personalized nutrition, and the rise of plant-based and alternative proteins. Additionally, the book examines the social dynamics of dining in the digital age, the transformation of culinary education, and the ethical considerations of technological advancements. Through a series of engaging chapters, readers will gain insights into the future of food sustainability, the influence of social media on culinary trends, and the role of technology in global food security. "The Robotic Gourmet" celebrates the balance of tradition and innovation, offering a comprehensive and thought-provoking exploration of how technology and sociology are redefining the culinary world. This book is a must-read for food enthusiasts, tech aficionados, and

CHAPTER 17: THE ROLE OF TECHNOLOGY IN SUSTAINABLE FOOD...

anyone curious about the evolving landscape of food and dining.

www.ingramcontent.com/pod-product-compliance
Lightning Source LLC
LaVergne TN
LVHW010442070526
838199LV00066B/6140